George F. Kennan and the
Origins of Containment,
1944–1946

GEORGE F. KENNAN
and the
ORIGINS *of*
CONTAINMENT,
1944–1946
The Kennan-Lukacs Correspondence

———————

GEORGE F. KENNAN AND JOHN LUKACS
Introduction by John Lukacs

UNIVERSITY OF MISSOURI PRESS
COLUMBIA

909.82
K34g

Copyright © 1997 by John Lukacs
University of Missouri Press, Columbia, Missouri 65201
Printed and bound in the United States of America

5   4   3   2   1   01   00   99   98   97

Library of Congress Cataloging-in-Publication Data

Kennan, George Frost, 1904–

    George F. Kennan and the origins of containment, 1944–
1946 : the Kennan-Lukacs correspondence / George F. Kennan
and John Lukacs : introduction by John Lukacs.

    p.   cm.

    Includes bibliographical references and index.

    ISBN 0-8262-1108-9 (alk. paper)

    ISBN 0-8262-1109-7 (pbk.)

    1. Kennan, George Frost, 1904–   —Correspondence.
2. World politics—1945–   .   3. United States—Foreign
relations—1945–1989.   4. Cold War.   5. United States—
Foreign relations—Soviet Union.   6. Soviet Union—Foreign
relations—United States.   I. Lukacs, John, 1924–   .   II. Title.
D843.K3947   1997
909.82—dc21   96-48659
                                                                    CIP

∞ ™ This paper meets the requirements of the
American National Standard for Permanence of Paper
for Printed Library Materials, Z39.48, 1984.

Designer: Mindy Shouse
Typesetter: BOOKCOMP
Printer and binder: Thomson-Shore, Inc.
Typefaces: Meridien

This Book Is Dedicated
to
ROBERT H. FERRELL

Contents

George F. Kennan and the Origins of Containment, 1944–1946

INTRODUCTION
by John Lukacs

———————

During the second half of the twentieth century the history and the development of the United States were dominated by the "Cold War" with Soviet Russia—more precisely, by the actuality of a political and by the potentiality of a military confrontation of these two giant states, the two remaining superpowers of the globe. This involved not only the foreign and military policy of the United States, that is, the course of the American ship of state; it had great effects as well on the development of the American people, on the structure of their society and their economy, and on the tendencies and categories of their political and ideological beliefs. Some of these effects were superficial and transitory. Many of them were enduring. (Consider only that the duration of the Cold War, from 1947 to 1989, corresponded to more than one-fifth of the entire history of the United States until then, and that it lasted almost three times longer than *all* the previous wars of the United States combined, including the Civil War.) It ended in 1989, with the retreat of Russian power from Central and Eastern Europe, exactly two hundred years after the birth of the United States, with the inauguration of George Washington as its first president.

So much for the duration and the, by and large, fortunate ending of the Cold War. What were its origins?

In both world wars of the twentieth century the United States and Russia, two distant Great Powers, were allies. During World War I their alliance was short and, for the most part, inconsequential: it lasted six months and ended with the Bolshevik revolution in St. Petersburg in November 1917. Opposing Communism, and even involved—marginally and briefly—in an attempt of military intervention against it, the American government, alone among the great powers of the world, refused to extend diplomatic recognition to the Soviet Union until 1933; but because both the United States and the Soviet Union—for very different reasons—withdrew from Europe for at least twenty years, in the 1920s and 1930s there was no actual conflict between them. During World War II, after June 1941, the United States and Russia became military and political allies. That alliance—at least on the military level—was an unavoidable necessity, since neither the American-British forces nor the Russians were capable of conquering Hitler's Third Reich by themselves. That much was recognized by their leaders, who agreed on one thing (and perhaps on one thing only): that in this war Germany must surrender unconditionally and at the end of the war, at least temporarily, be occupied in its entirety. In pursuit of this aim, the government of the

United States, and President Roosevelt in particular, preferred to postpone political and geographical questions—that is, both the extent and the conditions of a postwar Russian sphere of interest in Europe. The inclinations of the British government, and of Winston Churchill in particular, were different; but, despite his prestige, his power was no longer sufficient to convince his American allies to address themselves to these questions before it would become too late.

All of this began to change in 1945. On the one hand, American expressions and sentiments of goodwill for the Soviet Union were reaching their peaks then. The declarations signed by Roosevelt, Stalin, and Churchill at the Crimean (Yalta) Conference in February 1945 met with universal acclaim. The Soviet Union agreed to become a principal member of the United Nations organization. The meeting of American and Russian troops on April 25, 1945, in the center of Germany was a great symbolic event, signifying the appearance of two non-European powers in the middle of Europe, marking a division of it. In August 1945 Stalin, fulfilling a promise made to Roosevelt at Yalta, declared war on Japan—an event almost as important as that of the two American atom bombs, hastening Japan's decision to surrender. At the same time worrisome signs and portents of Stalin's intentions had not only begun to accumulate (definite indications of these had of course existed earlier, throughout the war) but had also begun to influence both the course of the American government and, here and there, currents of American opinion. Most of this involved Eastern Europe. It became evident, for example—and it was an important

example—that Stalin insisted not only on Russian terri-
torial gains at the expense of prewar Poland but also on
the establishment of a pro-Soviet and largely Communist-
dominated government in Warsaw, without free and un-
fettered elections in that country. Similar, though not ev-
erywhere identical, Russian policies were now apparent
in other states of Eastern Europe and in the Russian-
occupied zone of Germany. At the Potsdam Conference
in July 1945, the last "summit" of the three great war
leaders, some of these differences were discussed, but
nothing was solved or agreed upon, except for an un-
spoken acceptance of the status quo in Germany, that is,
of the economic sovereignty of the occupying powers in
their respective zones. Meanwhile the American government was also anxious about the agitation of Communist
parties and of their fellow travelers in some of the states
of Western and Southern Europe.

By the end of 1945 it was obvious that the Soviet-
American "honeymoon" (if that was what it was) was
largely over. What followed was a year of transition. The
foreign ministers' conferences in late 1945 and in 1946
and in early 1947 showed that on many important questions the United States and Soviet Russia were now opposed. Stalin in a speech in February 1946 suggested the
existence of a protracted conflict of Communist Russia
with the capitalist powers. The at times gradual, though
essentially unrelenting, Russian pressure on the Eastern European states in order to ensure their entire sub-
servience to Moscow was more and more obvious. That
an "iron curtain" was now descending across Europe,
from the Baltic to the Adriatic, was stated by Churchill in

his speech in Fulton, Missouri, in March 1946—a state-
ment with which the Truman administration did not yet
associate itself but which it did not entirely disavow either, since the evidence was stark and real. There were
places, here and there, where American pressures contributed to a Russian retreat (in northern Iran in early
1946, for example), but these were few and far between.
The possibility of a further Russian, or Communist, expansion in Europe (and also elsewhere) could no longer
be discounted.

Early in 1947 the British Labor government asked the
American government to relieve it from the onerous task
of actively sustaining the Greek government in its civil
war against Communist Greek bands in the north. President Truman rose to the challenge and went to Congress
with the request to commit the United States to the defense of Greece and also of Turkey (which, too, was oc-
casionally threatened by Soviet Russia). This so-called
Truman Doctrine of March 1947 was then followed by
the announcement of the Marshall Plan in June 1947,
whereby the United States was underwriting the economic reconstruction of most of Western Europe, in view
of the dangers of Communism among other reasons. The
offer of this benevolent American intervention in the affairs of Europe was extended to Eastern Europe and Russia, too, but it was rejected by Stalin and by his satellites on
his orders. The division of Europe (and of Germany) was
nearing completion. In early 1948 the last partially democratic Eastern European government in Czechoslovakia
became fully Communist-dominated; later in that year
the governments of two contrasting Germanies emerged;

and the Russians tried to eliminate the West from Berlin through a blockade of West Berlin's inhabitants. By that time *Cold War* had become an accepted term among the American people.

To contain Russia and Communism from expanding further in Europe had become the dominant principle of American foreign policy. The term *containment* was employed by George F. Kennan, then director of the Policy Planning Staff of the Department of State, in an article in the July 1947 issue of *Foreign Affairs,* under the pseudonymic sign of "X." Ever since that time Kennan has been regarded as the architect of "containment," a policy and an ideology discussed and described at innumerable times and occasions during the last fifty years. Yet the "X" article was not the beginning but the culmination of a process that had begun more than a year before. From the above it should appear that the crucial phase of the turning from a pro-Russian to an anti-Soviet policy was that from its first signs in mid-1945 throughout the year 1946. To most of this the present small volume will be devoted, wherein it will also appear that the crucial turning point in Kennan's career occurred not in July 1947 but in 1946, leading to the subsequent rise of his influence.

As Alexis de Tocqueville wrote, democracies have definite disadvantages when it comes to their foreign policy, because of the constant interference by and the preoccupation with domestic policies in their statecraft. Even more incisively, he wrote that—contrary to the accepted opinion of his time—in a democratic nation the movements of public opinion are not inordinately rapid but, to the contrary, inordinately slow. In 1945 many Americans still regarded Soviet Russia as their nation's principal ally. Two years later both government leaders and the majority of public opinion saw in Soviet Russia the principal enemy of their country. That was of course a reaction to the crude evidences of Stalin's brutal tactics; but it was a complex phenomenon. The only comparable instance was the turn of the American people, from August 1914 to April 1917, from a national mood of self-satisfaction with absolute American neutrality to the national inclination for a decisive American intervention in a European war. That transformation of opinions and sentiments had taken almost three years. The transformation from World War II to Cold War took a year and a half. It was a revolution in American state policy—as well as American public opinion—that has had few precedents in the history of the Republic.

George Frost Kennan was born in 1904 in Milwaukee. After graduating from Princeton University he entered the Foreign Service of the United States. His first assignments to Eastern European capitals served the purpose of perfecting his knowledge of Russian affairs and of the Russian language, even when there were no official diplomatic relations between the United State and the Soviet Union. In 1934 he was posted to Moscow as third secretary of the first American embassy to the Soviet Union, led by Ambassador William C. Bullitt. Thereafter his postings included Vienna, Prague, and Berlin, with corresponding advances within the hierarchy of the Foreign Service. In 1944 he was returned to Moscow as minister-counselor, under Ambassador Averell Harriman. The breadth of his knowledge, his diplomatic abilities, and the quality of his character had already impressed some people in Washington, but there was no reason to expect that beyond an honorable and well-deserved career in its Foreign Service he would be destined to perform a great service, let alone play an important role, in the history of the United States.

All of this would suddenly change in 1946; but before describing that, something ought to be told about the mentality of George Kennan, which was unusual and perhaps even unique at that time. While he did not believe in the merits of that extreme—and largely abstract—isolationism that had marked much of American foreign policy in the 1920s, he had profound doubts about the merits of the extreme—and also largely abstract—internationalism that marked much of American public thinking especially in the later stages of World War II. His wide knowledge of history and of foreign affairs made him skeptical of ideologies that would leave the limits of American national interests undefined. More specifically, he was deeply and personally concerned with the widespread evidences of ignorance and illusions about the Soviet Union, apparent not only in important instruments of public opinion but also among people in high positions (as in the case of Joseph E. Davies, American ambassador to Moscow at the time of Stalin's purges). He was also aware of the limited, though insidious, influence of Communist sympathizers in a few government departments.

Kennan was serving as first secretary in the American embassy in Berlin when Germany invaded Russia in June 1941. In a letter to Loy Henderson (referred to in this volume) he expressed his concern about the validity and the consequences of an American political alliance with the Soviet Union, a state that, because of its character, was not a "fit ally" of the United States. After being posted to Moscow again, in 1944, he felt compelled to draft a long paper, entitled "Russia—Seven Years After," warning his potential readers of illusions about the nature and ambitions of Stalin's government. What he had feared, he thought, had happened: he knew that his paper would be read by few people of influence; more important, he knew that the attitude of both government and public opinion concerning the Soviet Union was marked by a compound of undue illusions, undue thoughtlessness, and unduly short-range military and political considerations.

Still—as mentioned above—by 1945 some of these attitudes had begun to change (including those of Ambassador Harriman in Moscow), although the realization of a new course of American policy had not yet crystallized. Then came the event of Kennan's Long Telegram of February 22, 1946, which must be described in some detail. It was very ably summed up by Richard Snow, the editor of *American Heritage,* in his brief introduction to "From World War to Cold War."* In February 1946 Kennan was alone in Moscow, temporarily in charge of the embassy (Ambassador Harriman was away). He had

> received a routine request from the Treasury Department, which wanted him to explain some instance of Soviet intransigence about the World Bank.

American Heritage, January 1966, pp. 42–43.

"The occasion, to be sure, was trivial," Kennan wrote in his *Memoirs,* "but the implications of the query were not. . . . It would not do to give them just a fragment of the truth. Here was a case where nothing but the whole truth would do. They had asked for it. Now, by God, they would have it."

It took the form of an eight-thousand-word telegram—"all neatly divided, like an eighteenth-century Protestant sermon, into five parts. (I thought that if it went in five sections, each could pass as a separate telegram and it would not look so outrageously long.)" The wire laid out the "Kremlin's neurotic view of world affairs," concluding that although "impervious to the logic of reason," Moscow was "highly sensitive to the logic of force. For this reason it can easily withdraw—and usually does—when strong resistance is encountered at any point."

The reception was all that Kennan had wished, and more. Indeed, the Long Telegram became the founding document of the policy of "containment," the cornerstone on which the West built its Cold War strategy.

To this I must add that—in one important sense—Kennan was abashed by the reception of his message in Washington. Yes: the Long Telegram was immediately reproduced and circulated on the highest levels of the government. Yes: soon he was called to Washington, where he was then appointed director of the Policy Planning Staff, a new post of considerable importance. "It changed my career and my life in very basic ways." But he was abashed by the character of its reception; more precisely, by the fact that not only the validity of his arguments but the very willingness of people to read or hear or to listen to them was wholly dependent on their timing*— typical, alas, of the lamentable tendency of a large modern democracy to lack foresight on the one hand and to depend on current mental climates on the other.

Another sixteen months passed until Kennan's famous "X" article on "Containment" appeared in the summer of 1947. That is the main reason, and justification, for the publication of this correspondence, which deals mostly with the years 1944 to 1946 and not with 1947—that is, with the antecedents and origins of "containment," rather than with another analysis of the "containment" thesis itself, the effects and the consequences of which were largely predictable in 1947, even as its interpretations were, and continued to be, arguable.** When, in late 1994, the editor of *American Heritage* suggested an article in which I would interview George Kennan concerning his reminiscences about the origins of the Cold War, I agreed, "but with one proviso: Because 'both Kennan and I are believers in (and practitioners of) the primacy and the accuracy of the written word,' the interview would take the form of an exchange of letters." (Those six letters are part of a precious bulk of correspondence between George Kennan and myself, going back now for forty-five years.) Before their publication they were edited and here and there abbreviated by both of us. The letters are coherent and telling enough to speak by themselves. At the same time there remain historical questions and

*About this see below, pages 24–25, 36–38.
**About this see below, pages 60–61, 68–72.

problems that are either alluded to in them or form their background; and for the sake of both students and general readers I will attempt to elucidate them further within this Introduction.

One matter—if not perhaps the most important one—in this exchange of letters may be especially significant, because it is contrary to most of the accepted ideas about the origins of the Cold War—on the American side, that is. Beginning about 1961, so-called revisionist historians, journalists, and publicists have argued that the American reaction to the Soviet Union in 1945, 1946, and 1947 was unduly impulsive and unduly hasty. (Some of them have gone so far as to attribute the American decision to use the atom bomb to the intention of impressing Stalin.)* The more orthodox interpretation eschews such arguments by stating that the United States was hardly, or not at all, responsible for the origins of the Cold War (which is largely true) and that its response to Stalin's dangerous ambitions was made at the right places and at the right time. Yet both Kennan and the present writer agree that the attempt to limit and define the extent and the conditions of a Soviet sphere of interest in Europe should have been made considerably *earlier* than in 1947.

This will appear in the first exchange in these letters; but there are two other historical conditions that this

---

*For the most telling and detailed analysis and criticism of the shortcomings—historical, intellectual, personal, and moral—of such writers, see Robert James Maddox, *The New Left and the Origins of the Cold War* (Princeton: Princeton University Press, 1973).

correspondence could not discuss in detail, even though they are considered at various points.

One is the factor of American public opinion. It is a most complicated and difficult subject, for many reasons.* A principal problem is the dependence of a democratic government not only on what public opinion is but also on what it seems to be. Another principal problem is what we may call the momentum of public opinion. We have seen that American goodwill to the Soviet Union was reaching its peak in early 1945,** at the time when at least a few people at the highest levels of the government began to have serious anxieties about Russia. It is because of this slow but enormous accumulation of a momentum of opinion*** that the reactions of a government, instead of being influenced, let alone governed, by foresight, are often distressingly slow. This is a condition involving not only politic calculations but also an, alas, only too frequent unwillingness of leaders to seem "ahead" of public opinion—something that eventually results not in an

---

*Consider that "public opinion research" in 1945 was only in its infancy (George Gallup had founded his Institute of Public Opinion Research in 1935)—not that it has reached a stage beyond a confusing and presumptuous adolescence even at this time of writing.

**See the chapter "A Sketch of the National Mind: American Public Opinion (and Popular Sentiment) in 1945" in John Lukacs, *1945: Year Zero* (New York: Doubleday, 1978).

***Consider how Marx's entire theory rests on his thesis of the Accumulation of Capital. Had he only considered the—sometimes more insidious, and almost always more powerful—phenomenon of the Accumulation of Opinion!

overestimation but in an underestimation of the capacity of people to respond. But then "public opinion" itself, in spite of its apparent pervasiveness, is an inchoate and undefinable phenomenon. For one thing, it is not identical with what may be called "popular sentiment." This is not the place for a disquisition of the difference between these two terms—except to say that this is relevant to a historical study of the 1945–1947 period. For instance, the war against the Japanese was even more popular than the war against the Germans among the American people at large. There were also considerable elements of the population—many Catholics, former isolationists, certain ethnic groups, and Republicans—whose views of Communism and of Russia did not conform to the views propagated and represented by the leading newspapers, books, magazines, radio shows, and films. Their opinions began to surface in 1945; because of the evidences of Soviet behavior in 1946 they seemed to be increasingly vindicated. (The result was not entirely salutary. It soon led to a national identification of anti-Communism with American patriotism, and not only to the attendant misinterpretation of Stalin's intentions but also to a wrong diagnosis of the global situation, according to which the main threat to the United States was international Communism, and not Russia's enlargement of her sphere of interest.) There are reasons to think that a realistic American foreign policy, concerned with Russian ambitions, especially in Europe, would not have been devoid of popular (and of British) support in 1945, and perhaps even somewhat earlier. But such a policy was dismissed (at times contemptuously) by the main instruments and representatives of public opinion and rejected, at least for a considerable time, at the highest levels of the government.

The other matter, to which historians have hitherto devoted little attention, is that considerations about a division of Europe—unstated and unacknowledged, to be sure—had existed already before 1945, involving the highest levels of the government, including President Roosevelt. As early as 1943 there was evidence that Washington was definitely set on maintaining Italy within the American sphere of influence, keeping the Russians at arm's length when it came to the Italian political situation. As early as 1943 President Roosevelt wished to assert a future American presence in the occupation of Berlin. As early as 1944 Washington showed its concern with the prospects of Communism in France, underestimating General de Gaulle's will and his ability to restrain the influence of Communists in the postwar government of France. At the same time the military, the Department of State, and the president were both suspicious and unwilling to listen to any of Winston Churchill's projects and warnings against an undue extension of the Russian sphere of influence in parts of Eastern and Central Europe. Indeed, when in December 1944 British troops were sent to Greece to subdue a violent Communist insurrection, London was publicly criticized by Washington (though, significantly, not by Moscow). As in the case of "public opinion," we face here another problem of terminological inexactitude involving "Washington" and "government." "Washington" and "government" functioned on different levels, at times in the service of differing purposes. High officials and emissaries of the president and of government included men such as Harry Hopkins or Henry A. Wallace (who until September 1946 was a member of the Cabinet), men who were inclined to give Stalin the benefit of doubt and who subordinated almost everything to the aim of American-Soviet amity and mutual understanding. Yet there were important functionaries such as James V. Forrestal or Allen W. Dulles who as early as 1944 were anxious to restrict Russian influences where in their opinion they ought not belong. In between such representatives of differing tendencies lay the vast and inchoate mass of the "government," both unable and unwilling to question the accepted ideas of the day, or to acknowledge what was happening: the division of Europe into spheres of interest, and what these spheres of interests were to mean.

Whether George Kennan was right in 1941, that the United States, while giving military aid to Russia, could—and should—have avoided what de facto became a political alliance during the war, is being debated in this correspondence. But what is indubitable is that by 1945 his thoughts about the Soviet Union and about the necessary constraints of American-Russian relations had crystallized on three levels. One was his realization that a Russian predominance in most of Eastern Europe could not be avoided, in part because American power and influence had their limits; but he was convinced that the United States should not paper over the fact of such a division of Europe by meaningless declarations. The second was his conviction of the need to recognize that, all of the wartime comradeship notwithstanding, Russia continued to be ruled by a Communist tyrant who was both suspicious and aggressive, fearful and brutal, wherefore his empire must be contained within its existing and unduly swollen limits. The third recognition, consequent to the second, was that such a containment must not only mean an American commitment to the defense of non-Soviet Europe but that it would also, sooner or later, lead to a withdrawal of some of the most extended positions of Russian armed presence in Eastern and Central Europe, whereafter serious discussions about a correction of the division of Europe (and of Germany) would be proper.

Of these three recognitions only the second was generally accepted by the American government in 1947. One of three is of course better than none; and, in the long run, "containment" worked. The political climate in 1947 had become such that people were now very receptive to Kennan's judicious exposition of the character of Soviet Communism, though much less so to his long-range considerations: they were receptive to ideology rather than to geographical realities. That overwhelming and categorical ideological tendency then contributed to what Kennan soon came to deplore: to the emphasis on the military character of "containment," and to the subsequent and protracted unwillingness of the Western governments and, *primus inter pares,* of the United States to consider, let alone discuss with Moscow, the possibility of a renegotiation of the division of Europe. Yet it was the anti-Communist Kennan, the architect of the Containment Policy, who first dared to advocate such a consideration only a few years after the division of Europe and of Germany had hardened into an ugly physical reality. By that time he had resigned from the government (more exactly, his resignation was suggested to him by Secretary of State John Foster Dulles in 1953); and his subsequent proposals were dismissed and disregarded by men who had been his allies and associates in 1947.

This is not the place, nor is it the purpose of this Introduction, to follow with a survey of Kennan's career after 1947. There are, however, two remaining matters that do belong within the current purview—together with the summary recognition due to the exceptional achievements of his historianship (including his willingness to engage in this kind of lengthy correspondence in the ninety-second year of his life).

One of those matters is his rejection of anti-Communism as if that were identical with American patriotism. Unlike many intellectuals, other commentators, and public figures, Kennan was never influenced by Marxism, regarding it as an ideology that was not only immoral but resting on an entirely inadequate conception of human nature. Precisely because of that fallibility Kennan never saw it as the fundamental and unchanging principle explaining Soviet Russian behavior. The irony is that this was precisely how many people understood the Containment argument. But more is involved here than the misinterpretation of the text of a seminal article. After its publication the way was open for Kennan to assume the mantle of an intellectual leader of anti-Communism. Yet both his view of the world and the probity of his character led him to oppose the extreme anti-Communist ideology that seemed to threaten the decency and the stability of American public life. He made this evident in public addresses as early as 1951 and again in 1953, at the height of the Cold War and of the popular surge of the McCarthy period. His subsequent advocacies for dealing realistically with Russia made many people and scholars question—many of them to this day—the consistency of his personal and political philosophy. Yet he was more consistent than were many of his critics, since his advocacies and admonitions rested on certain fixed principles rather than on mutable ideas.*

These principles may be summed up as follows: (1) States and nations were more fundamental realities than were their professed ideologies. (2) It was improper for the United States to commit itself to the expansion of democracy (whatever that meant) all over the world.** (3) It was proper for the United States to maintain diplomatic relations with Soviet Russia, without threatening the integrity of the Russian state itself, while the latter must not actively threaten the existence of states vitally important for the national interests of the United States. (4) Because of its own interests the Soviet Union did not want a war with the United States, a condition that, with

*About principles and ideas see below, pages 60–61. In this respect Kennan's position was not unlike Churchill's, whose concern with the extent of Russia's expansion in 1944–1945 was rejected by the American governmental and military establishment, notably by General Eisenhower, as being unduly anti-Russian—by the same Eisenhower (and many of the same people) who in 1953 after the death of Stalin rejected Churchill's proposal to attempt a renegotiation of the division of Europe with Moscow as being unduly pro-Russian.

**Consider that in 1956 Section Nine of the platform of the Republican Party called for the establishment of American sea and air bases "all around the world."

all of the requirements of a prudent statecraft in mind, the American government ought to recognize. (5) This was especially so in the now present, and potentially immensely dangerous, time of atomic weapons.

The other matter that belongs here is the still ongoing conflict between two different views of the Cold War—indeed, of the entire history of this century. According to one, held by many "conservatives" and "neoconservatives" (the quotation marks are intentional) "history changed gears" (the phrase of the political thinker James Burnham, often repeated by others) with the Russian Revolution in 1917. Thereafter the history of the world was dominated by the struggle between Communism and Capitalism, or call it Totalitarianism and Democracy, the first incarnated by the Soviet Union, the second by the United States, at least from 1917 to 1989, during which protracted struggle the Second World War was but an erratic chapter. According to the other, the two main events of the twentieth century were the two great world wars, the mountain ranges in the shadows of which we have lived, until 1989 at least: one of the many results of the First World War having been the Russian Revolution in 1917, and a result of the Second World War the Cold War between Russia and the United States. The two world wars were the great catastrophes undermining Western civilization, with tremendous and manifold consequences, of which Communism in Russia was but one. That is the view of both George Kennan and of the writer of this Introduction, who makes bold to say that neither Kennan nor he has an iota of doubt about its historical correctness.

THE KENNAN-LUKACS CORRESPONDENCE

December 20, 1994
JOHN LUKACS TO GEORGE KENNAN

———————————

We both agree that the two mountain ranges that marked the historical landscape of the twentieth century were the two world wars and that Communist aggressiveness and its dangers were consequences of them. In 1917 the Bolshevik seizure of power in Russia was but a consequence of the First World War, and in 1947 the beginning of the Cold War was a consequence of the Second World War. By now hundreds of books and studies exist about the origins of the Cold War. But what interests me is something of the years 1945 and 1946, the passage from the Second World War to the Cold War. For during that time we may discern a revolution in American attitudes and opinions, and not only in the course of the great American ship of state. In 1945 the government, the military, and the leaders of American public opinion saw the Soviet Union as the principal ally of the United States. Yet by the spring of 1947—months before the publication of your famous

"X" article in *Foreign Affairs* expanded on the thoughts in the Long Telegram—all these elements saw the Soviet Union as the principal opponent, indeed enemy, of the United States.

That was not a geopolitical necessity (as many people saw it, including Hitler). It was a natural and often overdue reaction to Stalin's actions—more precisely, to how he interpreted the division of Europe. I write "overdue," contrary to the so-called revisionists and to others too, who argue that the American reaction in 1947 was immoderately hasty. I for a long time have thought that the opposite was true: that an American attempt to define the conditions—geographic, even more than political—of a postwar Russian sphere in Eastern Europe, preferably through an agreement with Stalin, should have been made much earlier. You may or may not agree with me about this, but what really interests me is not the undue *haste* but the undue *lassitude* of Washington and of public opinion. And here I come to a most telling passage from volume 1 of your *Memoirs,* your description of the reception of the Long Telegram you sent on February 22, 1946.

Twenty-one years later you wrote: "The effect produced in Washington by this elaborate pedagogical effort [that ironic phrase was meant to emphasize your own criticism, in retrospect, of some of the rhetoric in it] was nothing less than sensational. It was one that changed my career and my life in very basic ways. If none of my previous literary efforts had seemed to evoke even the faintest tinkle from the bell at which they were aimed, this one, to my astonishment, struck it squarely and set it vibrating with a resonance that was not to die down for many months. It was one of those moments when official Washington, whose states of receptivity or the opposite are determined by subjective emotional currents as intricately embedded in the subconscious as those of the most complicated of Sigmund Freud's erstwhile patients, was ready to receive a given message. . . . Six months earlier this message probably would have been received in the Department of State with raised eyebrows and lips pursed in disapproval. . . . Six months later, it would probably have sounded redundant, a sort of preaching to the convinced. This was true despite the fact that the realities which it described were ones that had existed, substantially unchanged, for about a decade, and would continue to exist for more than a half-decade longer. All this only goes to show that more important than the observable nature of external reality, when it comes to the determination of Washington's view of the world, is the subjective state of readiness on the part of Washington officialdom to recognize this or that feature of it."

Almost fifty years after these events, and more than a quarter century after you wrote the above passage, do you still think that it was "subjective emotional currents" that "determined" that reception at that time? Were there not some political calculations, including calculations of what goes under the inchoate category of "public opinion" at work too?

January 18, 1995
GEORGE KENNAN TO JOHN LUKACS

———————————

In thinking about your question, I have a hard time distinguishing between my own opinions and those of the governmental establishment in Washington and of the public at large; but I shall give you, for whatever they are worth, my impressions of the states of mind that prevailed in all those quarters.

So far as my own opinion is concerned (and this was probably the least important of the three), you will agree, I think, that this was fairly adequately described in my *Memoirs*, particularly if there be taken into account not only later recollections but also the papers, at that time highly confidential, that I wrote from the embassy in Moscow between 1944 and 1946. The one of these papers that has received the least attention from historians but was actually basic to the understanding of the later ones was the first of them, written in September 1944 and entitled "Russia—Seven Years Later." My purpose in writing this paper, while only gently brought forward in the content of it, was to express the shock I experienced upon returning to service in Russia after an interruption of some seven years. The shock was occasioned by the realization that the Soviet regime with which I found us to be dealing in 1944, and from which we had come to hope for so much understanding for our aims in the war against Germany, was still indistinguishable from the one that had opposed in every way our policies of the prewar period, that had entered into the cynical nonaggression pact with the Germans in 1939, and that had shown itself capable of abominable cruelties, little short of genocide, in the treatment of large portions of the population from the areas of Poland and the Baltic states it had taken under its control.

I entered upon my work as Averell Harriman's deputy in Moscow in 1944, in other words, painfully aware that a massive misunderstanding was already establishing itself in the minds of American governmental leaders on the subject of the character of the regime with which they were dealing in Moscow, and that this, if not corrected, portended serious disillusionment and unpleasantness at some time in the near future.

Mr. Harriman had looked to me only to administer the staff and the routine day-to-day operations of the American embassy in Moscow, in order to relieve him of the necessity of occupying himself with anything else than matters of highest wartime policy, and he did not expect from me, nor did he, I suspect, particularly welcome, any expressions of my own views on problems of wartime policy. But I continued, as gently as I could (for anything beyond this might have produced highly negative and self-defeating reactions on his part), to remind him that the regime we were dealing with in Moscow was one whose aims for the postwar world were far different from our own. Seeing things this way, I naturally deplored the many manifestations of our professed high admiration for the Soviet leadership and of our belief that if we could only play up handsomely enough to Stalin's supposed tender sensibilities, we would find that leadership to be grateful partners in the approach to the problems of the post-hostilities period.

I was of course aware of the high degree of dependence of our war effort on the great contribution the Soviet armed forces were then making to the defeat of Hitler and of the necessity of giving them such small but effective military support as we could. But I had, after all, when serving in the Berlin embassy earlier in the war, written a personal letter, two days after the launching of the German attack on Russia in June 1941, to the deputy chief of the European division in the State Department, my friend Loy Henderson, warning about mistaking the significance of this great event. If we were "to welcome Russia as an associate in the defense of democracy . . . I do not see," I wrote, "how we could help but identify ourselves with the Russian destruction of the Baltic states, with the attack against Finnish independence, with the partitioning of Poland . . . , with the crushing of religion throughout

Eastern Europe, and with the domestic policy of a regime which is widely feared and detested throughout this part of the world and the methods of which are far from democratic."

I continued: "The Russian involvement in this struggle is not the result of any concern for the principles underlying the Allied cause. . . . Russia has tried unsuccessfully to purchase security by compromising with Germany and by encouraging the direction of the German war effort toward the west. . . . It has thus no claim on Western sympathies; and there is no reason apparent to me why its present plight should not be viewed realistically at home as that of one who has played a lone hand in a dangerous game and must now alone take the moral consequences. Such a view would not preclude the extension of material aid wherever called for by our own self-interest. It would, however, preclude anything which might identify us politically or ideologically with the Russian war effort."

What I found upon arrival in Moscow in 1944 was that this warning had been totally ignored. We were doing precisely the things I had urged that we not do.

My return to Moscow in 1944 coincided closely with the Normandy landings, the success of which disposed of the painful issue of a Second Front. But it did little to relieve our leaders of the fear that the Soviet leadership might decide to make another deal with Hitler and withdraw from the war. Even though I thought this turn of events to be highly unlikely, I still did not dispute the necessity of continuing to give the

Soviet armed forces such outright military support as we could. But I saw no reason for coupling this with such elaborate courting of Soviet favor as was then going on, or for encouraging our public to look with such high hopes for successful collaboration with the Soviet regime after the war.

The issue, it seemed to me, came to a head with the behavior of the Soviet regime during the Warsaw Uprising of August 1944. Mr. Harriman was obliged at that time to call at once upon Stalin and Molotov and to solicit their agreement to the use of the military airfields we then maintained in the Ukraine for operations in support of the Polish fighters. The rejection of this approach by the two Soviet statesmen was cast in such arrogant terms that it struck me as nothing short of insulting. One has to bear in mind the situation that then existed. We had, after all, created the Second Front. Our troops were fighting, successfully, though not without heavy losses, on the European front in the war against Germany. The Russians had already liberated the entirety of their own territory that had been overrun by the Germans. What was now at stake was not the further repulse of a German attack on Russia but the question of what would be the political outcome of further advances of the Red Army into the remainder of Europe. The Warsaw Uprising was, I thought, the point at which, if we had never done so before, we should have insisted on a thoroughgoing exploration of Soviet intentions with regard to the future of the remainder of Europe.

Franklin Roosevelt had always opposed any attempt to air such problems in advance of the complete defeat of Germany, fearing that to do so might create political conflicts between the Russians and the Western European and American allies and thus weaken the Allied military effort. The reasons offered for this position were not unserious. But it seemed to me that the situation that had now come into being was such that a clarification of the Soviet political aims with regard to postwar Europe could no longer be delayed. If Soviet behavior in the light of the tragic effort of the Poles to free Warsaw from the Germans was any indication of what we might expect from the Soviet leadership after Germany's defeat, then it was a question in my mind (and I think it was beginning to be a question in Mr. Harriman's as well) whether we could afford to wait before having a real and intimate exploration of the postwar designs of the Soviet government.

In the light of this background, the changes that came over American official and public opinion in the immediate aftermath of Roosevelt's death and the ending of the war in Europe not only held no terrors for me but appeared in large part a belated vindication of views I had long entertained. But the American government was at that time, as it is today, a wide and far-flung institution, and it is worth the effort to inquire just where the distortions in the governmental approaches to Russia had their origins and how they came to be adopted.

In major problems of foreign affairs, particularly those that related closely to the war effort, there were in 1944–1945 two overwhelmingly important centers of authority in Washington. One was the White House, and the other was the body known as the Joint Chiefs of Staff. (The State Department had at that time long ceased to play any significant part in matters of wartime policy and least of all of policy toward the Soviet Union.)

Until the final days of his life, Franklin Roosevelt seems to have clung to a concept of Stalin's personality, and of the ways in which the latter might be influenced, that was far below the general quality of the president's statesmanship and reflected poorly on the information he had been receiving about Soviet affairs. He seems to have seen in Stalin a man whose difficult qualities—his aloofness, suspiciousness, wariness, and disinclination for collaboration with others—were consequences of the way he had been personally treated by the leaders of the great European powers. FDR concluded that if Stalin could only be exposed to the warmth and persuasiveness of the president's personality, if, in other words, Stalin could be made to feel that he had been "admitted to the club" (as the phrase then went)—admitted, that is, to the respectable company of the leaders of the other countries allied against Germany—his edginess and suspiciousness could be overcome, and he could be induced to take a collaborative part in the creation of a new postwar Europe.

I do not need to dwell upon the deficiencies of this concept of Stalin's personality. There were others who, if they had been consulted, could have told FDR that Stalin was a man whose professed friendship could ultimately be as dangerous as his hostility. One of the worst features of these unreal assumptions on Roosevelt's part was that they were coupled with an evident belief that his efforts to tame Stalin and to make him into "one of the club" could be successful only if they were unilaterally undertaken and were kept separate from any similar efforts on the part of the British, including Churchill. This caused FDR not only to reject all efforts on Churchill's part to achieve a joint Anglo-American approach to Stalin but even to place his own one-on-one encounters with Stalin ahead, in timing and in importance, of his comparable relations with Churchill. That these inclinations on FDR's part could only have been deeply hurtful to Churchill is obvious. Worse still, they could hardly have failed to appear to Stalin as welcome opportunities for the employment of his favored tactical device, which was to place his opponents at odds with each other and thus encourage them to employ in the resulting conflicts among them the energies that might otherwise have been employed against him. Altogether, these efforts, not only by FDR but by others on the American side as well, to achieve a special relationship to Stalin, even at the cost of demeaning the prestige and authority of the president's own Western allies, and Churchill in particular, stand as one of the saddest manifestations of the almost childish failure on FDR's part to understand the personality of Stalin himself and the nature of his regime.

So much for the White House and the civilian side of the American establishment of 1945. How, then, about the military establishment?

It is perhaps not too much to say that senior American commanders who came into contact with their Soviet opposite numbers in the course of our wartime association found their personal relations with their senior opposite numbers in the Soviet armed forces to be less troubled than their comparable relations with their British counterparts. Of particular importance were of course the relations between Gen. Dwight Eisenhower and his Soviet counterpart, Marshal G. K. Zhukov. But similar reactions were experienced by the senior figures in the other great arms of American military effort: the Navy and the Army Air Force. And senior American commanders continued to the very end of the war in Europe to be strongly affected by their admiration for the dimensions and power of the Soviet ground-force effort in Europe and by the fear that it might be terminated by some sort of a separate Soviet peace with Hitler if political differences between the Soviet leadership and the Western Allies came to be aired before the hostilities were over.

Most of those officers who were sent to the Soviet Union and were required to deal with the Soviet military and civilian bureaucracies on the spot gained quite different and far less reassuring impressions of the Soviet military establishment than those then current among their superiors in Washington. But the influence they exercised was not comparable to that of the major commanders, and it seemed to us, as civilian officials stationed in Moscow, that by and large the senior American military commanders, as assembled in the Joint Chiefs of Staff, were animated by a measure of confidence in their senior Soviet opposite numbers that departed from what we would have considered the requirements of strict realism. I have memories of being taken severely to task in a private meeting with Gen. Lucius Clay in Berlin in 1945 for what the general then viewed as the excessively anti-Soviet attitudes of the State Department. The military, I was given to understand, would have known far better than the diplomats how to create a collaborative relationship with the Russians. (Further experiences, I gather, changed the general's views on such questions.)

We come now to the reactions of the American public. Here I am probably one of the worst persons to be consulted. Until the late spring of 1946 I was out of the country, serving in Moscow, and I had only remote impressions of the various states of opinion on Soviet-American relations.

Shortly after returning to the United States in the late spring of 1946, I was sent by the State Department on a speaking tour to places in the Middle and the Far West, where I was to explain American policies toward Russia to presumably less-well-informed people in these provinces. This assignment was the result of a curious choice on the State Department's part, because I had been for years, as the department should have known, in marked disagreement with our official attitudes and policies. But the journey was instructive. I found audiences in the Middle West (I think particularly of one in my native city of Milwaukee) to be troubled, thoughtful, and patient listeners, but sharp ones. On the West Coast it was quite different. On the campuses and among the members of the various organizations that had been set up to "help Russia" during the war, people were taken aback and sometimes felt themselves unpleasantly challenged by the things I had to say. Particularly was this the case at the University of California in Berkeley. In Los Angeles, on the other hand, where I addressed a meeting that I recall consisted primarily of prominent businessmen, what I had to say about the Soviet leadership was received with such loud enthusiasm that I was myself slightly alarmed by the chords I had touched. Some of these chords, I now suspect, were ones that were soon to be played, and to no good effect, in the period of the McCarthyist hysterias.

My impression, gained by this experience, was that much of American opinion, at least in educated circles, was at that time bewildered and uncertain. People had been persuaded for years by our government that the peoples and government of the Soviet Union were our great and noble allies. Now, contrary reports and opinions were beginning to be heard. Some of the difficulties that had occurred during the San Francisco

Conference on the establishment of the United Nations had already begun to make people wonder whether the Soviet regime was quite what they had been encouraged to believe it to be during wartime.

I have several times had occasion to say that it never pays for our government to give false impressions to the American public with the view to enlisting its support for short-term purposes, because this always revenges itself later when it becomes necessary to overcome the wrong impressions one has created. I see the governmental attitudes of the period resulting in claims about our Russian allies that were at the best serious oversimplifications and for the most part something far worse than that: an instance of the abuse and distortion of American opinion by a political administration that thought at the time it was doing a worthy and useful thing.

Actually, my retrospective impression is that most of the American public of that day—so long as Americans were fighting the Germans—were prepared to go along loyally and patiently with the Roosevelt administration's efforts to enlist enthusiasm for the war in Europe. But for some reason, which warrants more attention on the part of the scholars than it has received, the war in Europe never enlisted the same sort of hysterical-chauvinistic reaction and support that had characterized the American participation in the First World War. The more general American reaction was one of "Well, we are told that it has to be done. All right, but let's get it over with." It is my impression that this attitude also prevailed extensively among the American fighting forces at that time.

All of this is important, because it meant that although American governmental wartime propaganda was for the most part unprotestingly accepted while the fighting was going on, there were always some reservations about it among common people. Thus the transition to a more sober and realistic view of the Soviet dictatorship and of world affairs generally was not as difficult as it would have been had public emotional involvement in the European war been far more intense than it actually was. It must be remembered, in this respect, that it was only toward the end of the war that information about the Nazi Holocaust was beginning to seep through to wide elements of the American population. And even where it did begin to penetrate people's consciousness, there was a tendency to doubt (and this was perhaps greatest on the part of the troops fighting in Germany) that the Holocaust had any great awareness or support among the German civilian population, as distinct from the Nazi regime itself.

January 25, 1995
JOHN LUKACS TO GEORGE KENNAN

Well, what you have now written to me is very interesting and important. It should impress those
who think (and teach and write) that the American
reaction to oppose the Soviet Union in 1947 was premature, or aggressive, or impulsive, or hasty. But this
correspondence is about 1945 and 1946, not 1947—
though I will have to return to 1947 in one single
instance. And now there are two or three passages in
your letter that perhaps we could discuss further.

You warned in your June 1941 letter to Loy Henderson against "anything which might identify us politically or ideologically with the Russian war effort." But
are "politically" and "ideologically" the same matters?
We know something that we did not know in 1941,
and that is the somber realization that for all their
might, the British and the American empires would
not have been able to subdue the Third Reich without
the enormous contribution of the Russian armies. That

that contribution did not occur for the purposes of world democracy is obvious. But this was a fact that you yourself had once mentioned: that as early as 1939 the game was up, since the British and the French could not hope to defeat Germany without Russia (and America) in the field. And therefore, even with all the subsequent shortcomings of their view of Russia in mind, the president's and the Joint Chiefs' conclusion of Rainbow 5 in the spring of 1941 was not only correct but decisive: that in the event of a two-front war, Atlantic and Pacific, the subduing of Germany would have to come before that of Japan. What of course is interesting and significant is what you just wrote about American popular sentiment (I write "popular sentiment" rather than "public opinion"), with which I of course agree: Unlike the priorities of Rainbow 5, the war against Japan was more popular among the American people than the war against Germany. And again, you yourself wrote that Roosevelt's reasons were "not unserious" when he opposed any possible confrontation with Stalin, since that would weaken the Allied military effort.

I would go further: not only "weaken" but "endanger" seriously. After all, Hitler was not a madman. Ever since November 1941 he knew that he could not win his war. But that did not mean that he would accept defeat. From that time on (and his model in this respect was Frederick the Great from 1757 to 1761) his policy was to fight so tough that at least one of his enemies would realize the hopelessness of subduing him, whereupon that unnatural coalition of capitalists and communists would break up. (And break up it did, but too late for him.) So while I agree with you that the dangerous eventuality of a new German-Russian accommodation may have been exaggerated, it could not be ignored; consequently an American policy that would have suggested, openly or tacitly, an unwillingness to agree to what was de facto a political alliance with the Soviet Union during the war could have been very dangerous.

But then, I agree, September 1944 should have been a kind of turning point. For two reasons at least. One, after the success of the Normandy invasion, and with the massive presence and advance of American-British armies in Western Europe, Stalin could no longer argue that Russia was bearing the overwhelming brunt of the war. Two, by that time, especially in Poland (but also in the Balkans), the nature of his postwar ambitions had become starkly evident. And that was, by and large, ignored by the president and by the military and government leaders. They were unwilling to face that prospect (or even think about it—and the president's illness and his habitual tendency to procrastinate mightily contributed to that), while public opinion was unprepared for it ideologically. That was partly, but only partly, the fault of the government. And this is one of the deepest problems before historians of the democratic age: the propagation and the formation and the momentum of ideological currents is one of the most difficult things to reconstruct, in part because its evidences are fragmentary, complicated, and yet enormous in their extensiveness.

That is why I must expatiate on what you write about Roosevelt's tendency to demonstrably disassociate himself from Churchill and the British. What was at work there, I think, were not only Roosevelt's political calculations but ideological elements. In his ideological—and, in a way, historical—view (and in this he was entirely in accord with much of public opinion and with Washington) he saw the United States "in the middle"—by which he meant in advance of both the admirable but nevertheless antiquated and still largely Tory Britain, as represented by Churchill, and the rough, pioneer, and socialist "democracy" of the Soviet Union, perhaps a representative of some kind of a future—and that world democracy would eventually lead to some kind of a convergence. He was unable to see that the Soviet Union represented something entirely different (and also backward). I think that what was at work here was not only the customary *unwillingness* but an obvious *inability* to think and see correctly. In this Roosevelt was not alone. There was, for example, Eisenhower, the politician general par excellence, who in 1944 and 1945 was suspicious of Churchill for being unduly worried about the Russians, if not altogether anti-Russian, the same Eisenhower who in 1953 and 1954 would dismiss Churchill as insufficiently worried about the Russians, if not altogether pro-Russian.

I think that the declarations at Yalta and the arrangements at Potsdam only confirmed Stalin's view that while the Americans might not say so openly, what was happening in reality was a division of Europe. Perhaps America's great omission was not so much an absence of toughness with the Russians as the old American tendency to not consider geography seriously enough. That the Russians would be the dominant power in Eastern Europe was unavoidable. But that the actual limits of their dominion should be established in accord with the Allies, and as soon as possible, was not the American policy (though it was Churchill's), that, for example, Bulgaria or Romania or prewar eastern Poland were one thing, while Hungary, Austria, and Czechoslovakia were another—that, alas, was not considered.

March 2, 1995
GEORGE KENNAN TO JOHN LUKACS

You question whether FDR and the Joint Chiefs of Staff were not fully justified in concluding that anything less than a virtual political alliance with the Soviet Union would seriously jeopardize the Western military effort.

My answer would be no.

That we would have to give the Russians such military support as we could for their efforts to resist the German attack was clear. But I saw no need for us to conceal the very serious differences in our political purposes. Our attitude toward the Soviet leaders, as I saw it, should have been: "We know that you did not enter this war of your own volition. Neither did we. We have no reason to believe that your long-term aims are similar to, or even compatible with, our own; and we cannot, in the absence of searching political discussions with you, commit ourselves to the public approval of whatever uses you are likely to make of your military victory. We are prepared to put aside the long-term conflicts of our interests in present circumstances and to give you such support as we can in the liberating of your own territory from German control and in the ultimate frustration and defeat of the German war effort. All this being understood, let us deal with each other in a correct and businesslike way, and may the relationship be characterized by mutual respect, as befits association in a common military task. But please do not expect us to pretend that your long-term aims are anything other than what we have known them to be. And do not expect us to mislead our population or the rest of the world by creating the impression that you and we are genuine long-term allies, fighting for similar ultimate political ideals."

I suspect that the Russians would have seen the logic of this and would have respected the nature of the relationship thus described. And the same, I think, would have been the case with regard to our own people, had the matter been frankly explained to them.

You ask whether Stalin did not interpret the discussions and results of the Yalta and Potsdam conferences as evidence that we Americans, whatever we might say publicly, were really prepared to recognize and give tacit acceptance to a division of Europe and Germany along the high-water marks of the Soviet and Western military advances into the continent. You may indeed be right about this. My own position, consistent with the view put forward above, was of course that since we were not in a position to challenge the Soviet occupation of that portion of Europe that had fallen to Moscow's authority by virtue of these advances, we should regard these advances for the moment as a fait accompli and should concentrate on the internal strengthening of the remainder of Europe but that, at the same time, we should avoid giving any political or moral endorsement to the uses the Soviets were likely to make of the preeminence they had now acquired in the Eastern and Central European regions and particularly to the treatment they were obviously already giving to the subordinate populations. Our position should have been: "Under present circumstances we will avoid taking public positions on these matters. But don't ask us to assume any responsibility, moral or political, for the manner in which you are facing the responsibilities you are incurring in the territories you have overrun."

Now let me turn, once more, to the misunderstanding on the part of Franklin Roosevelt and much of his entourage on the question of Soviet aims for Poland and the remainder of Eastern Europe. Nothing, to my mind, served more to create confusion on this point than the credence given in both Britain and the United States to the thesis put out so insistently, as the war approached its end, by Soviet agents and Western fellow travelers, that all Moscow really wanted from the postwar Eastern Europe were "friendly governments." Coupled with this thesis was the allegation that regimes dominant throughout most of this region before the war had been not only "anti-Soviet" but fascistic, and that it was thus necessary that they now be replaced by ones that, in Moscow's view, could be considered "friendly."

Most of the countries in question were new ones—children, so to speak, of the peace settlements after World War I. Lacking any well-established traditions of democracy, they practiced, for the most part, little of what the term was taken to mean in Western countries. In some instances the leadership was conservative or right-wing—a circumstance that heightened in many Western liberal and left-wing eyes the plausibility of the Soviet claim that these governments were bad and reactionary and ought of course to be replaced by ones more "friendly" to the great socialist republic to the east, now fighting so bravely against the Germans.

Actually, most of those Eastern European regimes had many reasons, beyond just the ideological ones, for apprehension about their eastern neighbor. The situations of these countries during the war, with Nazi Germany on the one side and Soviet Russia on the other, had obviously been ones of great delicacy and danger. So searing had been their wartime experience that by the time the Soviet armies overran their territories all of them would have been happy enough to treat with courtesy and respect any Moscow policy that would recognize their professed friendship, accept their independence, and withdraw the occupation forces as soon as possible after the war.

But Stalin was not the man to accept such a relationship. Himself devoid of the capacity for loyalty, he had no confidence in the loyalty of others. He could believe only in the cynically professed "friendship" of persons and regimes wholly and abjectly under his authority. What this meant for the Eastern European peoples, when the war was over, was something that probably surpassed the imaginations of many people in the West. For what was at stake here was not just a prolonged and relatively benign military occupation, designed to assure that the subject country, while enjoying autonomy in purely domestic affairs, would not handle its foreign relations in a way that would jeopardize Soviet interests. There were, as most of the Soviet leaders knew, terrible skeletons in these particular closets; many tens of thousands of them in fact. When, for example, in the final months of the war, the Soviet forces reconquered Polish territory, the Soviet secret police, and Stalin personally, had a great deal to conceal. It is not surprising they were determined that there should never be a regime in power in Warsaw that would reveal these crimes. Nor is it surprising that Stalin should then have assigned to his police apparatus, as he appears to have done, the power to control not only all Polish affairs, internal as well as external, but those of the remaining Soviet-occupied countries as well—and this for years to come.

This, in effect, was what Franklin Roosevelt was up against, all unbeknownst to himself, in his futile effort at the Yalta Conference in 1945 to assure democratic independence for the Eastern European peoples by accepting, and trying in good faith to meet, what he took to be Stalin's demand for "friendly governments" in that part of the world. To this must be added the insistence of the military leaders in both the United States and Britain that everything possible be done to conciliate Stalin and to persuade him that the major Western powers were still his loyal allies and political supporters. It was the naive hope that this sense of camaraderie in a great common military endeavor would produce a fundamental change in Soviet attitudes and that collaboration with Russia would thus continue even into the postwar period. The Yalta Conference of February 1945 was the last of the summit meetings still outwardly dominated, at least on the American side, by the cultivation of this essentially fictitious and misleading scenario.

But while all this was happening, there was in progress a steady growth of disillusionment at lower levels of government in both Washington and London over the prospects for the future of Soviet-American relations. A number of things were happening in those final months of the war that were decidedly at odds with the thesis of a continuing Soviet-American collaboration. The experiences and observations of the American and British members of the tripartite commissions set up to assure the observance of the armistice terms in the former enemy countries of Eastern Europe were not only unfavorable but alarming. Stalin's initial reluctance to send Molotov as the Soviet representative to the ceremonies and negotiations attending the founding of the United Nations came as a severe shock, particularly to senior people in the State Department who had placed high hopes in Soviet support for the organization as an agency for stability in international life. And then of course, above all, there was the bitter question of Poland. In the immediate aftermath of the Yalta Conference it became abundantly clear that the Soviet leadership had no intention whatsoever to permit free elections or, indeed, democratic processes of any sort to prevail there.

How many of these difficulties came to the attention of Franklin Roosevelt in the weeks following the Yalta meeting is not clear. It is clear that the president was shocked and offended when Stalin, upon learning that American officials in Italy had been approached by German peace feelers, reacted violently (this was another instance when Stalin's pathological suspiciousness overcame him) and accused Roosevelt of trying to make a separate peace with the Germans behind his back and at Russia's expense. The president, for his part, reacted with no smaller indignation to what he felt had been a wholly unwarranted suspicion on Stalin's part. The matter had still not been fully cleared up when death overtook the president on April 12.

It is hard to know how much of all this had got through to Truman before Roosevelt's death. He had never been consulted by the president or even taken into confidence on problems of Soviet-American relations. But he had been a regular reader of official communications passing through the White House Map Room and must have picked up something of what was going on. And now, with Molotov arriving on a visit to Washington some days after his assumption of the presidential office, Truman did convene a gathering of persons from whom he thought he could expect guidance on how he should conduct himself. Most of those participating in this discussion had already been troubled by, or made aware of, the serious difficulties now arising in the Soviet-American relationship.

A number of tales have circulated about the rough reception Truman gave Molotov when the two of them met, the following day. Some of these stories were subsequently overdramatized by journalistic hearsay, but there is no doubt that the language Truman spoke to Molotov on that occasion was more businesslike, more serious, and more blunt than anything that either Molotov or Stalin were accustomed to hearing from American lips. In the ensuing weeks, to be sure, Truman somewhat softened his words, if not his attitudes, in his communications with the Kremlin. The influence of Harry Hopkins and others who for one reason or another had an interest in preserving some of the amenities of the earlier wartime relationship may have made themselves felt at this point. And Truman, in attending the Potsdam Conference of midsummer 1945, was anxious to be seen as not departing drastically from the line followed at the earlier Big Three meetings by his greatly more prestigious and internationally respected predecessor. He was still swayed by the atmosphere that had outwardly prevailed at those

earlier meetings so that we find him even affected by
the old assumption that success or failure in influencing
the Soviet side depended in large part on the question
of whether Stalin did or did not "like you"—or, as
the saying went, whether you could "get along with
Stalin."

But these concessions on Truman's part were no
more than superficial aspects of a wartime relationship
that, never solidly founded in the first place, was now
in reality deeply undermined. Altogether, the Potsdam
Conference, the last of its kind ever to take place, has
to be regarded in retrospect as a final, halfhearted, and
largely unsuccessful effort to preserve something of the
earlier wartime relationship. But from the time when it
became undeniably evident that the Soviet authorities
were determined to treat the European peoples overrun by the Red Army in a manner wholly unreconcil-
able with American hopes, these unreal expectations
could no longer be maintained.

This transition from one publicly held concept of
Soviet Russia as a friendly object on the horizon of
America's political perspectives to another and almost
totally contrary one was bound to be, for our government and public, a complicated, delicate, and in
some respects even perilous process. There was, in
particular, the danger that many people who had once
been assured that the future of world peace would
rest upon an enduring Soviet-American amity might
now rush to the opposite extreme (as indeed numbers
of them did) and conclude that if collaboration with

Russia was impossible, then war was inevitable. The main purpose of my own "X" article and of others of my public statements at that time was to assure these people that even though it was impossible to collaborate very extensively with Moscow, this did not mean that it was impossible to live without catastrophe in the same world with the Soviet Union. There was also the further danger that if the deterioration in Soviet-American relations was seen as a serious reversal in the fortunes of this country, many Americans would be vulnerable to the suggestion that this reversal was explicable only by the presence in the higher echelons of American government and society of traitors secretly doing the bidding of the Soviet Communist authorities.

The reality was, of course, that already before the outbreak of world war in 1939 the Western powers had simply not developed their own military strength to a point, or even to anything resembling the point, at which they could hope to defeat Hitler by their own efforts alone. The Soviet struggle against Hitler was not conducted by Moscow for the purpose of rescuing the Western powers from the situation into which their weakness had placed them, but it had this effect. And what has to be recognized was that there was, very naturally and inevitably, a price to be paid for this great Soviet contribution to the armed struggle, and this price took the form of the postwar domination of a large part of Europe, and this for years to come, by the Soviet Union. We and our Western European allies had only ourselves to blame for this tragic necessity.

Had these realities been explained betimes to the American people, the distortions in the official American view of the Soviet-American relationship during the wartime years and just thereafter might have been largely avoided, and the jolt of the transition to more realistic concepts in the immediate post-hostilities period might have been smaller and easier for the American political system to accept.

It is unfortunately a characteristic of democracies that their political establishments are incapable of looking far into the future, of recognizing long-term dangers, and of anticipating those dangers at early stages. To point this out is not to question their many other advantages or to suggest that there is any easy way by which these deficiencies could be overcome. But it is to argue that if these weaknesses cannot be remedied, then the peoples and governments of the Western democracies must learn to recognize that heavy prices have sometimes to be paid for their continued endurance.

April 23, 1995
JOHN LUKACS TO GEORGE KENNAN

I think that your summary discussion, in these letters, of the misconceptions by the American government, including FDR, about Stalin and the Soviet Union is a great contribution to historical knowledge. Many of its materials are there, of course, in your papers and in your *Memoirs;* but there, by necessity, they are only parts of a larger story, whereas here they are brought together. Equally important is how these misconceptions during the Second World War led to the development of the Cold War, or rather to the conditions along which it developed—*not* that the United States was the principal perpetrator of those conditions. I still do not *entirely* agree with you that the de facto alliance among the United States, Britain, and Russia during the war could have been avoided, or restricted to some kind of military cooperation, with America announcing not only to Stalin but to the world that (unlike Churchill's Britain) the United States would be loath to associate or coordinate its wartime efforts with Russia except in a circumscribed sense of military aid. The power of Germany was too large for that, and so were the consequent prospects of German policy to bring about a rift between its disparate opponents. But that is about the war itself and not about the 1945–1947 period with which this correspondence of ours is primarily concerned.

And on *that* we fully agree: What you have now written should make it definitely clear that, contrary to what so many critics of the Cold War have assumed, the American government's response to Stalin, at least in 1945 and early 1946, was belated rather than premature. What happened in 1946 was that finally those in charge of this country's world policy were catching up with you, and then, by and large, political and public opinion followed in 1947. When in July of that year, your now world-famous "X" article was published in *Foreign Affairs*, that was not the beginning but the end of a process, not only because the essence of the article was already latent in your Long Telegram in early 1946, and the "X" version actually delivered in your talk to the Council of Foreign Relations in early 1947, but because by July 1947 the change in the course of the giant American ship of state had been generally completed, largely in accord with your advocacies. Nearly a half-century later all kinds of people have recognized its merits: that the policy of containment has worked and that all honor is due its architect.

But it is not unusual—indeed it is often customary—for fine minds to be misunderstood. And while you may have been the architect of the policy of containment, the building contractors have not paid sufficient attention to your advice thereafter. But to show this would carry us well beyond 1947. What I wish to insist upon here (and perhaps elicit a final comment by you about it) is your consistency. It has been questioned by many people. Here is the George Kennan who before 1947 is so extremely wary of the Soviets, indeed, an architect of the Cold War, and soon thereafter the same George Kennan, during more than forty years, criticizes the anti-Soviet gestures and policies and the ideology of successive American governments as unrealistic and extreme. For forty years you were on occasion attacked and vilified, less from the left than from the right, by so-called conservatives—many of them ex-Communists—who referred to you as a man of illusions, for being unrealistic, at times even unpatriotic. I have, and always had, an answer to these fools. It may be summed up in a sentence that John Morley once wrote about Edmund Burke: "He changed his front; but he never changed his ground." Like Burke, you have never been an ideologue. Unlike so many public figures (including certain presidents, alas), you represented not ideas but principles. And those principles of yours rested not only on your knowledge of the world and of its history but on your deep concern with the inevitable limits of what this country can, or ought, to do.

So let me conclude this correspondence with two questions. The minor one is this: That a postwar conflict of interests between the United States and the Soviet Union could hardly have been avoided is obvious, but did not the sharpness of the confrontation arise from a reciprocal misunderstanding? By 1947 both the American government and a considerable portion of the public seemed to believe that having enforced Communist rule on Eastern Europe, Stalin was ready to advance into Western and Southern Europe, which was not the case. Conversely, Stalin believed that the Americans, having acquired their domination in Western and Southern Europe, were about to challenge his sphere of interest in Eastern Europe, which also was not the case. I wonder whether you see that in this way.

The other question: What were the sources of the previous (and successive) misunderstandings? Were they not the national inclination to think principally in ideological ways? Was this not the main reason, too, why you were often misunderstood by people who ought to have known better? Is there not a lesson latent in this, even now when we are facing a very different world, with very different dangers? All through your life you have been consistent in being aware of the limits—and consequently of the proper purposes—of the role of the United States in the world. These limits were not, and are not, imposed upon us merely by material conditions. You have been a consistent idealist and a realist, which is not at all contradictory but the best possible combination, since the opposite of the idealist is the materialist, not the realist.

April 28, 1995
GEORGE KENNAN TO JOHN LUKACS

A question you would like me to answer, if I have understood you correctly, was whether the Cold War was not the reflection of misunderstandings on both sides of the intentions of the other side, each ascribing to the other the intention to try to solve the division of the European continent by military means.

The answer is: Yes, of course, these military fears existed. On neither side were they justified.

Our fears of a Russian onslaught on Western Europe flowed in part from the rigidities of the American military mind (and others like it among our Western European allies), which yielded readily and extensively to the congenital military propensity to exaggerate the strength of any possible opponents while ascribing to them only the darkest of intentions. In addition to this there was the fact that we came out of World War II with a great military establishment that now had no visible major opponent. There was, I fear, something of this in the image of the Soviet Union that established itself in the American military establishment in the immediate wake of the Second World War and found its expression in the assumption that the Soviet leaders were determined to conquer Western Europe and establish subservient Communist regimes throughout it. This image promised to fill the vacuum just referred to, and to give it a new purpose, a new function, even in a sense a new legitimacy, to the greatly swollen military-bureaucratic establishment with which the end of the war had left us.

As for the Soviet suspicions of us and our leading Western European partners, these were aroused only gradually, but were eventually confirmed, to their satisfaction at least, by the entire trend of American policy in the immediate postwar years. The Soviets found reasons for these suspicions not only in our unwillingness to pursue with them any realistic discussions about the future of Europe but also in the increasingly obvious intention to rearm the West Germans and bring them into NATO membership. They, particularly Stalin personally with his congenital oversuspiciousness, could interpret these developments only as evidences of a determination on our part to drive them to the wall, to the abandonment of all the political fruits they thought they had earned, and to which they felt themselves entitled, by their recent war effort.

That all these fears and expectations on both sides were unsubstantial and unnecessary goes without saying. The members of the NATO pact could never have been brought together and mobilized for anything in the nature of an attack on Russia. Stalin and his henchmen should have recognized this.

As for our suspicions of them, I have already mentioned the insubstantial nature of the ones that prevailed in our military-political establishment. But there is one other reflection that in my own opinion would have reassured us greatly had we been willing to recognize its implications.

There was, by now, a widespread understanding among Americans that Soviet intentions with regard to Europe were irreconcilable with, and in that sense inimical to, our own. But how did they intend to implement those intentions? Many Americans jumped quickly to the primitive assumption that the Soviet aim was to overrun the remainder of Europe militarily and then to replace the governments there, including the West German one, with Communist puppet regimes. But if one had tried to look at this assumption from Moscow's standpoint, particularly from Stalin's, its unsoundness would have become immediately visible. Stalin had very good reason for rejecting any such course of action.

For one thing, it would have involved the unification of Germany under a single Communist government. But this was the last thing Stalin would have wanted to bring about. A German Communist regime, presiding over the entire population and commanding all the resources of the German state, could not have been expected to remain for long a puppet of Moscow. Such a Communist regime presiding over all of Germany would eventually occupy a position in world communism at least the equal of, or perhaps even superior to, that of any Russian Communist regime. But Stalin never forgot that to lose his preeminence in the world communist movement would be to endanger his position at home. He never doubted that the loyalty to himself professed by a great many senior Soviet Communists rested not in any great love for him personally but in the fear of him that he had himself inspired. And he had never been free of the fear that men of this ilk, chafing under the humiliations and dangers that attended their subordination to Stalin's tyranny, might find means of playing the international communist movement off against him, thus extracting themselves from his power and even occupying positions from which they could successfully oppose him.

If the center of European communism had moved to Germany, counterforces of great power and authority within the communist movement would, in short, have been brought to bear against the perpetuation of Stalin's personal tyranny in Russia. While sometimes the victim of his own diseased suspiciousness, Stalin was at other times nothing if not a realist, and his realism militated against any effort to bring the rest of Europe under control by force of arms. To be sure, he wanted a strong political position in Europe—this, for general reasons of prestige and influence. He would of course have liked to have, for example, a voice in the future development of the Ruhr industrial region.

But to try to bring this about by a great military on-slaught against the rest of Europe would have involved responsibilities and dangers he would never willingly have invited upon himself.

And this brings us, finally, to the question of ideol-ogy. It was, and still is, the view of many Americans that Stalin and the men around him were fanatical servants of radical Marxist ideology, as elaborated by Lenin. After all, it was in the name of this ideology that the Bolsheviks had seized power and that Russia had, as the world war ended, already been governed for some thirty years. The pretenses of the Soviet lead-ership, and the justification for all the sacrifices it had required from the Russian people, could be found only in the constant assertions of the validity of this system. Thus over the entirety of the Communist period in Russia, all discussions and decisions of official Kremlin policies had to be clothed in the curious rhetoric and ritualism of Leninist communism. And this spectacle could easily convince outsiders that the power of this ideology was the driving force of Stalin's own efforts and of the regime he headed, and of the spirit in which the Russian people had fought the war.

But this was not really the case. Up to the great purges of the 1930s it was true that many Russian Communists still thought and acted in response to ide-ological impulses. But the purges of the 1930s had largely destroyed these illusions. And enlisting the en-ergies and the devotion of the Russian people for the tremendous exertions of World War II had forced Stalin to shift the basic appeal from the ideological one to its nationalistic counterpart. So in the postwar period, although the vast majority of Russians were reconciled to the necessity, for reasons of prudence, of continuing to speak in ideological terms, the realities behind what they said would never again be primarily ideological. Nationalistic impulses were already the stronger force. And in Stalin's case there was then, as there had been even in the prewar decades, a decisive preeminence given to the cultivation and the protection of his great personal power. He too had no choice but to respect the rule that all decisions and discussions should be cast in the Leninist Communist rhetoric. There was no other conceivable rationale for his tremendous power. But he never had any great trust in his own personal-political environment. And there can be no doubt that the deepest and most decisive motivating force behind his words and his behavior was not really ideology but rather the protection of his absolute control over the movement and the country that he headed. Americans would have found it easier to understand Stalin, and to measure the possibilities of coming to terms with him, had they been willing to recognize the depth of this commitment.

Now one of your final questions is about my own consistency—of the consistency, that is, of the statements I made in the period from 1945 to 1947, compared with the positions I took throughout the Cold War.

Let me invite attention to certain things said in the paper (written, actually, almost precisely fifty years ago from the day I am now writing) entitled *Russia's International Position at the Close of the War with Germany* and included in the first volume of my *Memoirs*. In it I questioned Russia's capacity for living up to the responsibilities it had already assumed in Eastern and Central Europe. I voiced the view that Russian power was already overextended and expressed my doubt that Moscow would "be able to maintain its hold successfully for any length of time over *all* the territory over which it has today staked out a claim," in which case the lines of Russian power, I thought, "would have to be withdrawn *somewhat*." (This proved actually to be the case in Austria, in Finland, and in Yugoslavia.) If and when this limited retirement became necessary, I wrote, the Kremlin would use all its unpleasant devices of propaganda and vituperation to strengthen its position in the rest of the world. *But,* I went on to say, "Should the Western world stand firm through such a show of ill temper and should democracies prove able to take in their stride the worst efforts of the disciplined and unscrupulous minorities pledged to the service of the political interests of the Soviet Union in foreign countries, Moscow would have played its last real card. . . . Further military advances in the West could only increase responsibilities already beyond the Russian capacity to meet. Moscow has no naval or air forces capable of challenging the sea or air lanes of the world."

This should have sufficed, I think, to make it clear that I did not see our postwar contests with the Russians as being primarily military. No one who had given attention to these passages could have found in the X article a portrayal of the Soviet threat as chiefly a military one, calling for a similar response from us. (I was never told at the time what disposition had been made of this paper, which I simply submitted to the ambassador in Moscow, Mr. Harriman, who received it without comment and who never told me what, if anything, he did with it.) I did, however, frequently call attention to the basically hostile attitudes toward us of the Soviet regime under Lenin and Stalin and toward the noncommunist world generally, and I do not think that anything I wrote in the ensuing years reflected any change in my own opinions in this respect.

My differences with Washington policy became serious ones, from the Cold War standpoint, only in the final months at the end of my tenure as director of the State Department's Policy Planning Staff. They were occasioned, first, by my disagreement with the treatment of the problem of Soviet power in the now-famous governmental document entitled NSC-68, a paper with whose authorship my good friend and successor as head of the Planning Staff, Paul Nitze, was closely connected. But I was also greatly affected by Dean Acheson's almost contemptuous rejection of my urging that we should adopt a position of "no first use" with regard to the now-emerging nuclear weaponry. Neither of the lines of policy that actually flowed from these developments accorded with my own view of where the emphasis ought to be placed in our policies toward the Soviet Union. But there also was, beyond this, the question of our plans with regard to Germany and of the implications these held by our relationship with the Soviet Union.

I had always conceived that when we had made evident to the Soviet leaders that they had reached the real limits of the political expansion in Europe, the time would come when we would sit down with them and see whether we could not get their agreement to some sort of a workable understanding about the future of the continent. A central issue in any such discussion was bound to be the treatment of Germany. But it was clear that we would not be in a position to discuss this question in any promising way with the Russians if we had already committed ourselves to a line of policy, in relation to the part of Germany that was under our influence and control, that would clearly and not unreasonably be unacceptable to the Soviet side. Yet it was already becoming obvious, as noted above, that our government was planning not only to rearm Western Germany but to bring it into the Atlantic Pact. To me, such a policy meant in reality the congealing of the line of division through the center of Europe, and I felt bound to oppose it.

Whether or not I was right or wrong in these re-actions, I cannot see that they were in any way inconsistent with the warnings I had tried to give about the nature of Soviet power. The Russians had, after all, carried at least 80 percent of the enormous burden of defeating Hitler on the ground. That they were entitled to have some say in the question of the future of Central and Eastern Europe seemed to me obvious. But the only way to find out whether we could or could not come to some sort of an understanding with them that would reduce the growing military tensions and assure a more peaceful passage of Europe through the postwar period was to test them in reasonably private and realistic negotiations. If no agreement was possible, that was that; and then we would plainly have to face the consequences. But we would not know whether any such understanding was possible or not until we had talked with them. And this we were never willing to do. The sporadic public exchanges we had with them in the various foreign ministers' meetings, with both sides figuratively talking largely out the window to the world public outside, were mere propaganda exercises on both sides and did not qualify, in my view, as serious negotiations.

So I still see no inconsistency between the views I held in 1945 and those that I put forward in later years.

BIBLIOGRAPHY

Acheson, Dean. *Present at the Creation: My Years in the State Department.* New York: Norton, 1969.

Alperovitz, Gar. *Atomic Diplomacy: Hiroshima and Potsdam, the Use of the Atomic Bomb and the American Confrontation with Soviet Power.* 1965. Updated and expanded version. New York: Elisabeth Sifton Books, Penguin, 1985.

Anderson, Terry H. *The United States, Great Britain, and the Cold War, 1944–1947.* Columbia: University of Missouri Press, 1981.

Backer, John N. *The Decision to Divide Germany.* Durham: Duke University Press, 1978.

Blum, John Morton. *From the Morgenthau Diaries: Years of War, 1941–1945.* Boston: Houghton Mifflin, 1967.

———. *The Price of Vision: The Diary of Henry A. Wallace.* Boston: Houghton Mifflin, 1973.

Bohlen, Charles E. *Witness to History, 1929–1969*. New York: Norton, 1973.

Brooks, Lester. *Behind Japan's Surrender: The Secret Struggle That Ended an Empire*. New York: McGraw-Hill, 1968.

Buhite, Russell D. *Decisions at Yalta: An Appraisal of Summit Diplomacy*. Wilmington, Del.: Scholarly Resources, 1986.

———. *Patrick J. Hurley and American Foreign Policy*. Ithaca: Cornell University Press, 1973.

Butow, Robert J. C. *Japan's Decision to Surrender*. Stanford: Stanford University Press, 1954.

Byrnes, James F. *All in One Lifetime*. New York: Harper, 1958.

———. *Speaking Frankly*. New York: Harper, 1947.

Calvocoressi, Peter, and Guy Wint. *Total War*. New York: Penguin, 1979.

Campbell, Thomas M., and George C. Herring. *The Diaries of Edward R. Stettinius, Jr*. New York: New Viewpoints, 1975.

Chase, John L. "Unconditional Surrender Reconsidered." In *Causes and Consequences of World War II*, ed. Robert A. Divine. Chicago: Quadrangle, 1969.

Churchill, Winston S. *Triumph and Tragedy*. Boston: Houghton Mifflin, 1953.

Ciechanowski, Jan. *Defeat in Victory*. Garden City, N.Y.: Doubleday, 1947.

Clemens, Diane Shaver. *Yalta*. New York: Oxford, 1970.

Cochran, Burt. *Harry Truman and the Crisis Presidency.* New York: Funk and Wagnalls, 1973.

Dallek, Robert. *Franklin D. Roosevelt and American Foreign Policy, 1932–1945.* New York: Oxford, 1979.

Daniels, Jonathan. *Man of Independence.* Philadelphia: Lippincott, 1950.

Davis, Lynn Etheridge. *The Cold War Begins: Soviet-American Conflict over Eastern Europe.* Princeton: Princeton University Press, 1974.

Deane, John R. *Strange Alliance.* New York: Viking, 1947.

DeSantis, Hugh. *The Diplomacy of Silence: The American Foreign Service, the Soviet Union, and the Cold War, 1933–1947.* Chicago: University of Chicago Press, 1980.

Dilks, David, ed. *The Diaries of Sir Alexander Cadogan, 1938–1945.* New York: G. P. Putnam's Sons, 1972.

Divine, Robert A. *Roosevelt and World War II.* Baltimore: Johns Hopkins University Press, 1969.

Donovan, Robert J. *Conflict and Crisis: The Presidency of Harry S Truman, 1945–1948.* New York: Norton, 1977.

Eden, Anthony. *The Memoirs of Anthony Eden: The Reckoning.* Boston: Houghton Mifflin, 1965.

Feis, Herbert. *The China Tangle: The American Effort in China from Pearl Harbor to the Marshall Mission.* New York: Atheneum, 1965.

————. *Churchill-Roosevelt-Stalin: The War They Waged*

and the Peace They Sought. Princeton: Princeton University Press, 1957.

―――. *From Trust to Terror: The Onset of the Cold War, 1945–1950.* New York: Norton, 1970.

Ferrell, Robert H. *Harry S. Truman and the American Presidency.* Boston: Little, Brown, 1983.

―――, ed. *Dear Bess: The Letters from Harry to Bess Truman, 1910–1959.* New York: Norton, 1983.

―――, ed. *Off the Record: The Private Papers of Harry S. Truman.* New York: Harper, 1980.

Fischer-Galati, Stephen A. *Eastern Europe and the Cold War: Perceptions and Perspectives.* New York: Columbia University Press, 1994.

Gaddis, John Lewis. *The United States and the Origins of the Cold War, 1941–1947.* New York: Columbia University Press, 1972.

Gimbel, John. *The American Occupation of Germany: Politics and the Military, 1945–1949.* Stanford: Stanford University Press, 1968.

Hamby, Alonzo L. *Beyond the New Deal: Harry S. Truman and American Liberalism.* New York: Columbia University Press, 1973.

―――, ed. *Harry S. Truman and the Fair Deal.* Lexington, Mass.: D. C. Heath, 1974.

Hammond, Thomas T., ed. *Witness to the Origins of the Cold War.* Seattle: University of Washington Press, 1982.

Harbutt, Fraser J. *The Iron Curtain: Churchill, America and the Origins of the Cold War.* New York: Oxford, 1986.

Harper, John Lamberton. *American Visions of Europe: Franklin D. Roosevelt, George F. Kennan, and Dean G. Acheson.* New York: Cambridge University Press, 1996.

Harriman, W. Averell, and Elie Abel. *America and Russia in a Changing World.* Garden City, N.Y.: Doubleday, 1971.

——. *Special Envoy to Churchill and Stalin, 1941–1946.* New York: Random House, 1975.

Herken, Gregg. *The Winning Weapon: The Atomic Bomb in the Cold War, 1945–1950.* New York: Knopf, 1980.

Herring, George. *Aid to Russia, 1941–1946.* New York: Columbia University Press, 1973.

Hewlett, Richard B., and Oscar E. Anderson, Jr. *A History of the United States Atomic Energy Commission.* Vol. I, *The New World, 1939/1946.* University Park: Pennsylvania State University Press, 1962.

Hillman, William. *Mr. President.* New York: Farrar, Straus, and Young, 1952.

Horowitz, David. *The Free World Colossus.* Rev. ed. New York: Hill and Wang, 1971.

Hull, Cordell. *The Memoirs of Cordell Hull.* 2 vols. New York: Macmillan, 1948.

Irye, Akira. *The Cold War in Asia.* Englewood Cliffs, N.J.: Prentice-Hall, 1974.

Isaacson, Walter, and Evan Thomas. *The Wise Men, Six Friends and the World They Made: Acheson, Bohlen, Harriman, Kennan, Lovett, McCloy.* New York: Simon and Schuster, 1986.

Jensen, Kenneth M., ed. *The Origins of the Cold War: The Novikov, Kennan, and Roberts "Long Telegrams" of 1946: With Three New Commentaries.* Washington, D.C.: United States Institute of Peace Press, 1993.

Kaiser, Robert B. *Cold Winter, Cold War.* New York: Stein and Day, 1974.

Kennan, George F. *The Decision to Intervene.* Princeton: Princeton University Press, 1958.

———. *Memoirs: 1925–1950.* Boston: Little, Brown, 1967.

Kimball, Warren, ed. *Churchill and Roosevelt: The Complete Correspondence.* Princeton: Princeton University Press, 1984.

Kuklick, Bruce. *American Policy and the Division of Germany: The Clash with Russia over Reparations.* Ithaca: Cornell University Press, 1972.

Kuniholm, Bruce Robellet. *The Origins of the Cold War in the Near East: Great Power Conflict and Diplomacy in Iran, Turkey, and Greece.* Princeton: Princeton University Press, 1980.

Lane, Arthur Bliss. *I Saw Poland Betrayed.* Indianapolis: Bobbs-Merrill, 1948.

Larson, Deborah Welch. *Origins of Containment: A Psychological Explanation.* Princeton: Princeton University Press, 1985.

Leahy, William D. *I Was There.* New York: Whittlesey House, 1950.

Levantrosser, William F., ed. *Harry S. Truman: The Man from Independence.* New York: Greenwood Press, 1986.

Lukacs, John. *A New History of the Cold War.* New York: Anchor, 1966.

——. *1945: Year Zero.* Garden City, N.Y.: Doubleday, 1978.

Lundestad, Geir. *The American Non-Policy towards Eastern Europe: Universality in an Area Not of Essential Interest to the United States.* Oslo: Universitetsförlaget, 1975.

Maddox, Robert J. *From War to Cold War: The Education of Harry S. Truman.* Boulder: Westview Press, 1988.

——. *The New Left and the Origins of the Cold War.* Princeton: Princeton University Press, 1973.

Mastny, Vojtech. *Russia's Road to the Cold War: Diplomacy, Warfare, and the Politics of Communism, 1941–1945.* New York: Columbia University Press, 1979.

McCagg, William O., Jr. *Stalin Embattled, 1943–1948.* Detroit: Wayne State University Press, 1978.

McClauley, Martin. *The Origins of the Cold War.* London: Longmans, 1983.

McCoy, Donald R. *The Presidency of Harry S. Truman.* Lawrence: University Press of Kansas, 1984.

McNeill, William H. *America, Britain and Russia.* London: Oxford, 1953.

Mee, Charles L., Jr. *Meeting at Potsdam.* New York: M. Evans, 1975.

Messer, Robert L. *The End of an Alliance: James F. Byrnes, Roosevelt, Truman, and the Origins of the Cold War.* Chapel Hill: University of North Carolina Press, 1982.

Miller, Richard Lawrence. *Truman: The Rise to Power.* New York: McGraw-Hill, 1986.

Miscamble, Wilson D. *George F. Kennan and the Making of American Foreign Policy, 1947–1950.* Princeton: Princeton University Press, 1992.

Murphy, Robert. *Diplomat among Warriors.* New York: Pyramid Books, 1964.

Paterson, Thomas G. *Soviet-American Confrontation.* Baltimore: Johns Hopkins University Press, 1973.

Paterson, Thomas G., and Robert J. McMahon, eds. *The Origins of the Cold War.* Lexington, Mass.: D. C. Heath and Co., 1991.

Perkins, Frances. *The Roosevelt I Knew.* New York: Viking, 1946.

Phillips, Cabell. *The Truman Presidency: The History of a Triumphant Succession.* New York: Macmillan, 1966.

Pogue, Forrest C. *George Marshall: Statesman.* New York: Viking, 1987.

Reynolds, David, ed. *The Origins of the Cold War in Europe, International Perspectives.* New Haven: Yale University Press, 1996.

Rose, Lisle A. *After Yalta.* New York: Charles Scribner's Sons, 1973.

———. *Dubious Victory: The United States and the End of World War II.* Kent, Ohio: Kent State University Press, 1973.

Rosenman, Samuel I., ed. *The Public Papers and Addresses of Franklin D. Roosevelt, Vol. XIII.* New

York: Harper, 1950.

Sainsbury, Keith. *The Turning Point: Roosevelt, Stalin, Churchill, and Chiang Kai-shek, 1943: The Moscow, Cairo, and Teheran Conferences.* New York: Oxford, 1985.

Samii, Kuross A. *Involvement by Invitation: American Strategies of Containment in Iran.* University Park: Pennsylvania State University Press, 1987.

Sherwin, Martin J. *A World Destroyed: The Atomic Bomb and the Grand Alliance.* New York: Knopf, 1975.

Sherwood, Robert. *Roosevelt and Hopkins: An Intimate History.* New York: Harper, 1950.

Smith, Gaddis. *American Diplomacy during the Second World War, 1941–1945.* 2d ed. New York: Knopf, 1985.

Smith, Walter Bedell. *My Three Years in Moscow.* Philadelphia: Lippincott, 1950.

Snell, John L. *The Wartime Origins of the East-West Dilemma over Germany.* New Orleans: Houser 1959.

Stephanson, Anders. *Kennan and the Art of Foreign Policy.* Cambridge: Harvard University Press, 1989.

Stettinius, Edward R., Jr. *Roosevelt and the Russians: The Yalta Conference.* New York: Doubleday, 1949.

Stimson, Henry L., and McGeorge Bundy. *On Active Service in Peace and War.* New York: Harper, 1948.

Thomas, Hugh. *Armed Truce: The Beginnings of the Cold War.* New York: Atheneum, 1987.

Thorne, Christopher. *Allies of a Kind: The United States,*

   Great Britain, and the War against Japan, 1941–
   1945. New York: Oxford, 1978.

Truman, Harry S. *Year of Decisions.* Garden City, N.Y.:
   Doubleday, 1955.

Tsou, Tang. *America's Failure in China, 1941–1950.*
   Chicago: University of Chicago Press, 1963.

Ulam, Adam. *The Rivals: America and Russia since World*
   War II. New York: Viking, 1971.

Unterberger, Betty Miller. *America's Siberian Interven-*
   tion. Durham: Duke University Press, 1956.

Vandenberg, Arthur H., Jr., ed. *The Private Papers of*
   Senator Vandenberg. Boston: Houghton Mifflin,
   1952.

Ward, Patricia D. *The Threat of Peace: James F. Byrnes*
   and the Council of Foreign Ministers, 1945–1946.
   Kent, Ohio: Kent State University Press, 1979.

Wheeler-Bennett, John, and Anthony Nichols. *The*
   Semblance of Peace: The Political Settlement after the
   Second World War. London: Macmillan, 1972.

Williams, William Appleman. *The Tragedy of American*
   Diplomacy. 1959. Rev. and enl. ed. New York:
   Dell, 1962.

Woods, Randall Bennett, and Howard Jones. *Dawn-*
   ing of the Cold War: The United States' Quest for Or-
   der. Athens: University of Georgia Press, 1991.

Yergin, Daniel. *Shattered Peace: The Origins of the*
   Cold War and the National Security State. Boston:
   Houghton Mifflin, 1977.

INDEX

About the Authors

George F. Kennan is one of the greatest diplomats in the history of the United States. A historian and author of many works, he is much admired for the exceptionally high standards his scholarship pursues.

John Lukacs is a historian of international reputation and the author of many books, including his most recent, *Destinations Past: Traveling through History* (University of Missouri Press).